The Best of Marjorie Standish

Chowders
Soups & Stews

Down East Recipes

Down East Books
camden • maine

5

Down East Books Camden • Maine

Table of Contents

Maine is soup and chowder country. From the days of the heavy black soup kettle with its contents simmering on the back of the old black cookstove, to the cutting edge of Now, we're for soups, stews and chowders.

There are quick and amazing ways to make soups, and we like the availability of these methods. Yet Maine cooks think in terms of longer cooking periods when they have a soup or stew in mind. There is an economical stability about these old recipes, and the richness and nutritional value cannot be overlooked.

A Maine housewife has various ways of using an extremely low heat to do long, slow cooking. She remembers hearing her grandmother tell about the fireless cooker she learned to make in Farm Bureau years ago for this kind of cooking. Even now, you are apt to find one tucked away under the eaves in an old farmhouse attic.

Her mother talked of the deep-well cooker of her electric range, where she could cook stews or soups overnight or all day at very low cost. Kitchens became more streamlined, ranges were built to fit. The deep-well cooker had to go.

Today's Maine housewife has a simmering heat available on her kitchen range. Or she is apt to have a deep cooker on her kitchen counter, a separate appliance where again she turns to all-day or all-night cooking with the lowest cost of operation she could wish.

This is our way of life, and with great pride we call up from the past and present old standbys and simple up-to-date recipes to whet the appetites of all ages in the future.

Marjorie Standish

Chowders

● It was with great pride we used Maine canned corn. No longer canned in Maine. Yet the canning industry was founded in Maine over a century ago when Isaac Winslow perfected the steam process which made possible the commercial canning of fresh foods.

Maine Corn Chowder

2 slices salt pork
1 small onion, sliced or diced
2 cups diced raw potatoes
2 teaspoons salt
$\frac{1}{4}$ teaspoon pepper
1 cup water
1 can Maine cream style corn
1 quart milk
Piece of butter

Use a good sized kettle. Place 2 slices salt pork in it and cook slowly over low heat until fat is "tried out." Remove pieces of salt pork, add onion and cook slowly until onion is yellowed. Add water, diced raw potato, salt and pepper. Cover and bring to steaming point. Lower heat and cook until potato is tender or about 15 minutes. Add corn. Add quart of milk. Some canned evaporated milk may be added for richness, if you wish. Taste for seasoning, add piece of butter and reheat slowly. Allow chowder to ripen for an hour to develop flavor. Serves 4.

● Betty Jackson of Portland has shared so many recipes with us over the years. This winter she sent this recipe for a hearty Broccoli Chowder that will delight cooks for use, year around.

Broccoli Chowder

2 cans chicken broth, about 10¾ oz. each
About 4 cups chopped broccoli
(fresh or frozen)
3 cups milk
1 cup light cream or use evaporated milk
Salt to taste
2 cups shredded Swiss cheese
or may use Cheddar
1 cup chopped ham
½ stick margarine

Pour chicken broth into a large saucepan. Add chopped broccoli. Cook 10 to 15 minutes or until tender. Add milk, cream, cheese, ham, margarine and salt.

Cover and simmer 15 minutes. Stir frequently. Be careful not to cook on too high a heat, nor too thin a pot. Check seasoning, may need black pepper. To reheat, it is best to use a double boiler.

This recipe makes 2½ quarts of chowder.

● I've had my fair share of judging recipe contests and am very grateful for the opportunity. Not so many years ago, the Maine Dairy Council sponsored Maine Grange Dairy suppers during June — Dairy Month. I recall that the first time we did it, 153 Maine granges entered this contest. Huntoon Hill Grange of Wiscasset won that first contest. Their main dish, which was strictly Maine, was for Lobster Chowder. It was the first time I had known of lobster being used in a chowder.

Lobster Chowder

6 to 8 tablespoons butter
2 small onions, minced
4 medium-sized potatoes, diced
Salt and pepper to taste
4 medium sized lobsters, or when cooked and picked out, enough to make 2 pounds lobster meat
2 quarts milk, warmed

Cook the onion and potato in one cup water in a covered pan until they are tender. Add cooked lobster meat that has been cut into smallish pieces. Add butter. Stir with a fork to mix together and cook about 3 minutes. Warm the milk, then add to the lobster mixture. Season to taste. Allow to mellow. Serves 6 to 8.

● This is Helen Richam's recipe. I delight in telling this story. Helen was the Home Service Advisor with Central Maine Power Co. in the Western Division with Lewiston as headquarters. Helen was the Company to me and everyone she contacted. I always told her, "Everything I know, I learned from you." It was our private joke. We worked together 10 years. This is my favorite recipe.

Fish Chowder With Old Fashioned Flavor

¼ pound salt pork, diced
2 onions, sliced or diced
4 cups potatoes, in small pieces
1 or 2 cups water
2 pounds fish fillets (haddock, cod or cusk)
1 teaspoon salt
¼ teaspoon pepper
¼ teaspoon Accent
2 or 3 cups whole milk
1 tall can evaporated milk

Fry diced salt pork slowly in bottom of heavy kettle until golden colored. Remove pork scraps and set aside. There should be about 3 tablespoons fat in the kettle. Add onions and cook until yellowed (but not brown). Add potatoes and enough water so it comes nearly to top of potatoes. Place fish on top of potatoes, sprinkle with seasonings. Cover, bring to a boil, then cook on low heat until potatoes are tender and the fish "flakes." Pour in both kinds of milk and allow to heat thoroughly but not boil. Serves 6.

If you do any stirring at all, be gentle, because fish should be in fairly large pieces, not flaked apart and certainly not "mushed."

Good old Maine custom dictates that reheated pork bits be scattered on top of chowder. But you may serve them in a separate dish in case someone votes against the idea.

Seafood Chowder

2 slices salt pork
1 small onion, diced
2 cups water or bottled clam juice
3 cups pared and diced potatoes
1 pound haddock fillets
Salt and pepper
½ pound scallops
1 pint chopped clams, or 2 cans minced clams
1 can crabmeat or
2 cups fresh lobster meat or
2 cups Maine shrimp
2 quarts milk, scalded
1 stick butter or margarine

Fry out salt pork in kettle, remove pork scraps and cook diced onion in fat gently. Add water or clam juice, potatoes, cover and cook about 15 minutes. Lay haddock fillets and fresh scallops on top of potatoes, simmer slowly just until fish "flakes" and scallops are done. It is best to quarter the scallops before placing them in kettle. If clams are uncooked, then they go into the kettle at same time. If canned clams are used, then they are added with crabmeat, cooked lobster meat and cooked shrimp. Add scalded milk, stick of butter or margarine. Taste for seasoning. This chowder will be enough for 8 to 10 people.

Once the chowder is assembled, the top of double boiler is excellent for keeping until serving time and leaves far less chance of any curdling or "separation." This holds for any stew or chowder where milk is involved.

● Salmon chowder is a traditional chowder in Maine. It harks back to days when meat was not always on hand and fresh fish not available. This recipe has filled a need in Maine since olden days. It might be a good idea for you to have a can of salmon in your cupboard, just for an emergency.

My husband, George, taught me to make salmon chowder.

Salmon Chowder

2 slices salt pork
3 or 4 slices onion, diced
3 cups diced potatoes
Salt and pepper
1 cup water
1 tall can salmon
1 quart milk
Lump of butter

Cook slices of salt pork until fat is "tried out." Cook onion until golden in fat after removing pork slices. Add water to kettle, add raw potatoes, salt and pepper. Cover kettle and bring to steaming point. Cook on low heat about 15 minutes or until potato is tender.

Use pink, medium or red salmon. The buying public has come to think of red salmon as the only first class salmon, but this is not the case. Pink salmon used in this chowder is delicious and a lot less expensive.

Break up canned salmon, removing skin and bones. Leave salmon in as large chunks as possible. Add salmon and liquor to kettle. Stir lightly, add milk. Add piece of butter or margarine. Taste for seasoning. If you prefer, a half stick of margarine may be used as the fat for cooking onion in place of the salt pork.

The longer this chowder ages, the better. You will like its pink color. Serve with common crackers if available.

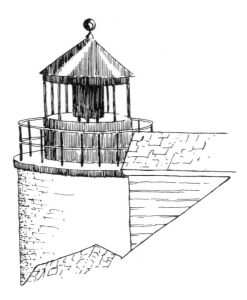

Maine Clam Chowder

1 quart fresh Maine clams, shucked raw
2 thin slices salt pork
1 small onion, diced in small pieces
4 cups diced (small) potatoes
1 cup water or enough to just show up through the potatoes
Salt and pepper
1½ quarts milk
1 tall can evaporated milk
Pieces of butter
Common crackers

Using a kettle, fry out salt pork, using a low heat. Remove pork and cook diced onion slowly in fat, taking care not to burn it. Add the four cups diced potatoes and the water; better add a little salt and pepper right now. Cover kettle, bring to steaming point, lower heat, cook until potatoes are soft, about 15 minutes.

In the meantime, using cutting board and a sharp knife, cut the head of each clam in two or three pieces. Do the same with the firm part of the clam and the soft part or bellies, also. No, I do not remove the black part. Save any juice you can.

When the potatoes are soft, stir in the cut clams, cover pan again, let cook for 3 minutes, no longer, for it toughens the clams. Add 1½ quarts of milk and the evaporated milk. Taste for seasoning, add salt and pepper if necessary. Keep in mind that as the chowder ripens it may be salty enough. Add piece of butter or margarine.

The old recipes always advised us to allow chowder to ripen in refrigerator several hours or a day; then to reheat it slowly over a very low heat. But now that we use homogenized milk, the ripening period often is omitted to avoid danger of the chowder separating, a problem sometimes associated with the use of homogonized milk. The use of evaporated milk, as given in these recipes, also helps to avoid curdling.

Serve chowder with common crackers, pilot crackers or Maine blueberry muffins. Serves six.

● Maine Style Clam Chowder is easily prepared from ingredients you have stored in your cupboard. It has a delicious flavor and you will exclaim, "This is second best to a chowder made with fresh Maine clams."

Maine Style Clam Chowder

3 slices salt pork
1 small onion, diced
1 8-ounce bottle clam juice
3 cups diced raw potatoes
Black pepper to taste
2 8-ounce cans minced clams or whole clams
3 cups milk or one 14½-ounce can evaporated milk, plus 1 can water
Salt to taste
½ stick butter or margarine

Using a deep saucepan, fry salt pork slowly, remove, and add diced onion. Cook on low heat until onion is soft. Add clam juice, diced raw potato and enough black pepper to satisfy your taste. Cover pan, bring to steaming point. Lower heat and cook at least 15 minutes.

Remove cover, add minced clams including juice, stir to mix. Cook about 10 minutes with cover off, allowing clams to simmer along in cooked potato mixture. Add milk, butter or margarine, heat to serving point. Taste for seasoning, add salt and more pepper as needed. Serves 4 to 6. If you wish, cut pieces of lightly browned salt pork into small bits and sprinkle on top of bowls of chowder before serving.

● Every once in a while you may be asked to help make clam chowder for a crowd. For many years Ruth Chase was the dietician at the Gardiner General Hospital, she developed this clam chowder recipe. It may be halved or quartered, depending on your needs. It is a fine recipe to have in your collection.

Clam Chowder For 100

6 quarts chopped clams
4 quarts clam broth
1 peck potatoes, pared and diced, small
2 pounds onions, peeled and diced
2 pounds butter
10 tall cans evaporated milk

Cook potatoes and onions in the clam broth. Heat milk (yes, these are the tall cans you buy in the market). Add butter. Then combine with tender potatoes and onions. Add chopped clams last. Season to taste with salt and pepper. No water added. There is some liquid in the chopped clams and with the bottled or canned broth, it is enough. Serve piping hot.

Soups

Vegetable Soup

soup bone
1 cup each diced celery, carrots, turnips and potatoes
1 small can tomatoes
1 cup each shredded cabbage and onions
¼ cup rice or barley
Salt, pepper, pinch sugar
½ bay leaf
1 tablespoon parsley
2 quarts cold water

Mix all the vegetables, seasonings, tomatoes and water together in a soup kettle. Wash rice and sprinkle over top of liquid. Place the soup bone in the kettle. Cover kettle. Bring to steaming point, turn to low heat and cook slowly for about 3 hours. Or longer, if that fits in better with your plans.

When you are ready to serve the soup, remove the

soup bone and add to soup any little particles of meat that might be clinging to it. The bits of meat make a richer soup. The soup is then ready for serving. Serves 8.

● When I started writing my column Cooking Down East in the late 1940's, one of the first recipes sent to me was for Potpourri Soup. A man from Dexter, Maine sent the recipe. He was in the insurance business. It is one of the most popular of my soup recipes. It may be made with hamburg or if you happen to have any — venisonburger.

Potpourri Soup

3 tablespoons butter or margarine
¾-pound hamburg or venisonburger
3 onions, sliced
⅓ cup barley
1 No. 2 can tomatoes

1½ quarts water
1 tablespoon salt
½ teaspoon black pepper
A few whole peppercorns, if you have them
3 carrots, sliced
3 potatoes, diced
3 stalks celery, diced
1 teaspoon steak sauce
1 teaspoon Worcestershire sauce

Using a large soup kettle, fry meat in melted fat until the red color leaves it, crumbling meanwhile so that meat is separated. Add onions and cook for a few minutes longer. Add water, tomatoes, barley, salt and pepper. Cover and simmer gently over a low heat for 1 hour.

Add vegetables, Worcestershire and steak sauces, bring back to steaming point, lower heat and cook for another hour. Serve hot with corn bread or hot biscuits. Makes 6 servings of ample proportions.

● Pea Soup was always served with johnnycake, and still is. After all, when you combine the economy of this rich wholesome soup with the solid comfort of johnnycake, you've got a real meal going.

Old-Fashioned Split Pea Soup

1 pound dried split peas, yellow or green
1 onion
1 carrot
1 potato
Salt
Pepper
2 quarts water

Wash peas and put in kettle; cut and add vegetables. Add seasonings and water. If ham stock is available, use some of that and 3 tablespoons of fat; otherwise, use a ham bone or smoked pork chop or ¼ pound salt pork. Cover kettle, bring to steaming point, lower heat and cook slowly for about 3 to 4 hours. Stir occasionally, to prevent scorching. Remove meat and fat. Strain soup, pressing vegetables through sieve, or use a food mill. Cut off any bits of ham or smoked pork chop if used and add to soup. Add 1 cup cold milk and reheat. Serves 6.

● Cornbread was made by the Indians before us, as everyone knows. Whether you call it cornbread or johnnycake (which I cling to), it was once upon a time called journeycake. No matter what you call it, this recipe for Spider Johnnycake is right to serve with Pea Soup. In Maine, when we refer to a spider, we mean a cast-iron pan with a handle, used for frying. Originally with legs, it was used over coals on the hearth. If you do not own a spider, then use an 8 x 8-inch pan for baking this johnnycake.

Spider Johnnycake

¾ cup cornmeal
¼ cup sifted flour
1 tablespoon sugar
½ teaspoon salt
1 teaspoon baking powder
1½ cups, plus 2 tablespoons milk
1 egg well beaten
2 tablespoons margarine

Sift dry ingredients. Add 1 cup plus 2 tablespoons of the milk and beaten egg. Mix only to dampen dry ingredients. Melt margarine in frypan or 8 x 8-inch pan. Turn mixture into pan, pour remaining ½ cup milk over batter. Do not stir. Bake at 400 degrees for 25 to 30 minutes. Serve piping hot. Serves 4.

Cream of Tomato Soup

4 tablespoons butter or margarine
3 tablespoons flour
2 teaspoons salt
A bit of black pepper
2 cups milk
2½ cups canned tomatoes
1 tablespoon minced onion
¼ teaspoon celery seed
½ teaspoon sugar
½ bay leaf
1 whole clove
⅛ teaspoon baking soda

Melt butter or margarine in a double boiler, then add flour, 1½ teaspoons salt, and the pepper. Blend. Add milk; stir until thickened. Meanwhile cook together the tomatoes, onion, celery seed, remaining ½ teaspoon salt, sugar, bay leaf and clove for 5 minutes. Strain, add soda, then add to thickened milk mixture gradually, while stirring constantly. Heat 1 minute, continuing to stir. Serves 4 to 6.

● You will want to refresh your memory with this recipe for Tomato Bisque. It's strictly Maine-ish. You will recall your mother used to make it, and it will be good to acquaint your own family with this easy-to-make soup.

Tomato Bisque

2 cups canned tomatoes
4 cups milk
4 tablespoons butter or margarine
Pepper
Salt
1 teaspoon sugar

Put tomatoes in a saucepan, juice too, chop tomatoes into small pieces. Add the butter, sugar, pepper and salt, bring to a boil. Boil about 5 minutes. Add milk and bring again to a boil. Serve as is, without straining. Don't ask me why it doesn't curdle, but it doesn't. Serves 6.

Cream of Potato Soup

2 cups small diced, pared, raw potatoes
2 minced medium onions
2 stalks celery, including leaves, diced
2½ cups boiling water
4 tablespoons butter or margarine
3½ tablespoons flour
1½ teaspoons salt
¼ teaspoon black pepper
2 cups milk
1 tablespoon minced parsley

Cook potatoes, onions, celery in the boiling water, covered, until very tender. Meanwhile melt the butter in top of double boiler. Add flour, stir until smooth; then add seasonings and milk. Cook while stirring until smooth and thickened. Then rub the potato mixture, liquid and all, through a sieve. You should have 3 cups puree. Add to sauce with parsley; heat and serve. Serves 6.

● Making-do has been the slogan of Maine cooks as far back as anyone can remember. It could be the reason sturdy Maine vegetables have been used as the basic ingredient in many soup recipes. Baked Bean Soup for instance. There is every reason for using left-over baked beans when the soup is so delicious. Or Parsnip Stew, which really isn't a stew at all; more like a chowder. If you have never made it, you should and learn why our forebears decided it was a cherished way of using parsnips. Best of all, Cream of Potato Soup was yet another way of producing a hearty soup from Maine's best known vegetable.

Baked Bean Soup

2 cups leftover baked beans, juice and all
2 cups water
1 large onion, peeled and quartered
2 cups canned tomatoes, undrained
1 tablespoon butter
Salt and pepper to taste

Put beans, onion and water into kettle and simmer slowly for 1 hour. Remove from heat, and rub all through a sieve or use a food mill. Return to kettle, add tomatoes to bean mixture, and simmer 1 hour longer. Season to taste with salt and pepper and add butter. Serves 4. This is good reheated.

Stews

Beef Stew

2 tablespoons fat
2 pounds chuck, rump or bottom of round
8 small onions, peeled
½ cup diced celery or 2 teaspoons celery seed
4 sprigs parsley minced,
or 2 teaspoons parsley flakes
1 bay leaf
2 tablespoons salt
¼ teaspoon pepper
3 tablespoons catsup
2 quarts boiling water
6 pared medium carrots
6 pared small potatoes

Melt fat in bottom of deep kettle. Remove gristle from meat, cut into 1½ inch cubes, roll in flour and brown in fat using a medium heat. Add 2 quarts of water, onions, celery, parsley, bay leaf, salt, pepper and catsup. Stir to mix ingredients. Cover and bring to steaming point. Reduce heat and simmer for 2 hours or until beef is tender.

Leave potatoes whole, cut carrots in half, add to stew. Cover and bring back to steaming point, reduce heat and cook slowly for another hour.

Using about 6 tablespoons flour, mix with cold water (prevents lumping) and when vegetables are tender, stir lightly into stew to thicken it. This stew serves 6 people.

● It happened when Horace Hildreth was Governor of Maine. Maine cooks were asked to submit their favorite seafood recipes.The response was heart-warming. I was one of the judges for that contest. It was the sort of happening one could never forget. This Crabmeat Stew was a winner then and it still is.

Crabmeat Stew

2 tablespoons butter
6 small soda crackers
2 cups fresh crabmeat
½ cup water
1 quart milk
Salt and pepper
1 tall can evaporated milk

Melt butter slowly in kettle. Roll crackers until crumbs are as fine as flour. Place these crumbs and the crabmeat in butter, add water, and let the mixture bubble for one minute to bring out the luscious flavor of the crabmeat. Pour in the milk and stir until it is very hot, but do not boil. Add seasonings and evaporated milk. Reheat, but again do not boil. Serves 6.

Lamb Stew

2 pounds boned lamb shoulder
$\frac{1}{4}$ cup flour
2 teaspoons salt
$\frac{1}{4}$ teaspoon pepper
3 tablespoons margarine
$1\frac{1}{2}$ quarts boiling water
1 peeled clove garlic
3 medium carrots, pared and quartered
2 medium onions, peeled and quartered
3 pared large potatoes, quartered
1 medium turnip, pared and sliced
$\frac{1}{2}$ cup diced celery
$\frac{1}{4}$ cup chopped parsley
1 teaspoon bottled thick condiment sauce

Remove any fat and gristle from lamb, cut meat into 1-inch cubes. Place flour, 1 teaspoon of salt and pepper into paper bag; shake lamb cubes in this. Brown meat in melted margarine in a Dutch oven or deep kettle until well browned. Add boiling water and garlic, cover and simmer for 30 minutes.

Then add the carrots, onions, potatoes, turnips, celery, remaining teaspoon salt, some more pepper, and simmer, covered, for 1 to 1½ hours longer or until meat and vegetables are tender. Remove meat and vegetables to a hot platter and keep hot. Add condiment sauce to liquid left in Dutch oven or kettle. Thicken with a flour paste of ⅓ cup flour mixed with ⅔ cup water. Pour over meat and vegetables. Sprinkle parsley over all. Serves 6.

Clam Stew

For each portion use 1 dozen small, tender Maine clams shucked out raw and 1½ cups milk. Saute clams in frying pan in their own juice, adding butter. Heat milk in top part of double boiler. Combine sauted clams and milk. Season to taste. Serve immediately.

Maine Lobster Stew

Boil 2 one-pound Maine lobsters and remove meat immediately, saving also the tomalley (or liver), the coral and the thick white substance from inside the shell. Using a heavy kettle, simmer the tomalley and coral in ½ cup butter for about 8 minutes. Then add lobster meat cut in fairly large pieces. Cook all together slowly using a low heat for about 10 minutes. Remove from heat or push to back of stove and cool slightly. Then add very slowly, 1 quart rich milk, stirring constantly. Allow the stew to stand, refrigerated, 5 or 6 hours before reheating for serving. This is one of the secrets of truly fine flavor. It's called aging. Serves 4.

You do not need salt or pepper when the stew is prepared in this manner. For the perfect lobster stew, stirring is the most important thing in this masterpiece, otherwise it will curdle. According to experts on fine Maine cookery, the important steps to success in creating the perfect lobster stew are, first, this partial cooling before ever so gently adding the milk — a mere trickle at a time. The constant stirring until the stew blossoms a rich salmon color under your spoon and, finally, the aging, since every passing hour improves its flavor. Some "experts" even say two days, overnight is good and 5 to 6 hours improves its flavor considerably. Be sure to reheat slowly.

Oven Beef Stew

2 pounds stew beef
2 tablespoons margarine or salt pork fat
Flour to dredge beef
1 tablespoon salt
¼ teaspoon pepper
4 cups hot water
¼ cup catsup
1 bay leaf
2 large onions, peeled and quartered or sliced
6 carrots, pared and quartered
4 medium potatoes, pared and quartered
1 cup diced celery

Cut beef into 1-inch cubes. Put flour, salt and pepper into a paper bag, shake up beef in bag. Melt fat in heavy pan with tight-fitting cover. This beef stew may be cooked on top of stove if you wish, but when done in the oven, it takes on almost a different flavor. Brown beef in melted fat. Add sliced onions, celery, catsup, bay leaf and hot water. Cover pan and place in 300-degree oven for 2½ hours. Add carrots and potatoes, replace cover, continue in oven at 300 degrees for 1 to 1½ hours longer, making certain the vegetables are tender.

Mix about ⅓ cup flour with ⅔ cup cold water, allow to set; then when Oven Beef Stew is ready, add flour mixture to thicken. Return to oven, cover off, to be sure flour is cooked. Serve in soup dishes or bowls. Serves 6, generously.

● Another Shrimp Stew recipe is amazing, not only in the ingredients but the manner in which it is made. It will serve 4 people. It is another friendly recipe for it came from our friend Joyce Matthews in Winslow.

Shrimp Stew

Using our Maine shrimp in a stew is a fine way of preparing this delicacy. because we like to serve these shrimp at their best, it is wise to use raw shrimp in making a stew for the best flavor. Maine shrimp do not need to be deveined.

Used peeled raw Maine shrimp, cook in butter just as you would in making any Maine stew. Do this slowly, the shrimp are cooked when they lose their glassiness and curl up. This takes 2 or 3 minutes.

Add milk slowly. Heat to boiling point, add salt and pepper to taste.

● This really isn't a stew at all, but you will like its name and the ease with which you may prepare it.

One-Two-Three Stew

1 package dehydrated onion soup mix
2 cans cream of mushroom soup, plus ½ cup water
3 pounds lean stew beef, cut in cubes

Combine all ingredients, cutting down on amount of dry onion soup mix if you like. Turn into large, buttered casserole. Cover. Bake for 3 hours at 300 degrees or 4 hours at 250 degrees. This amount serves 8.

New Shrimp Stew

1 can Campbell's cream of potato soup
fill can with milk
1 8-ounce pkg. cream cheese
1 can small shrimp

Soften cream cheese. We prefer using a 3-ounce package of cream cheese. Combine softened cream cheese with can of cream of potato soup. Add can of milk. Stir well. Add can of small shrimp. Heat and serve. Use double boiler. Serves 4.

Scallop Stew

1 pound scallops
¼ cup butter
1 quart milk
Salt and pepper to taste
½ tablespoon Worcestershire sauce

Melt butter in soup kettle, cut raw scallops in bite-size pieces, cook slowly in melted butter. They are cooked as soon as they turn white. Remember to cook all fish "short," overcooking toughens all fish. Add milk slowly, stirring as you do so. Add Worcestershire sauce, salt and pepper to taste. Heat. Keep in mind that a scallop stew is a little on the sweet side, yet a delicious stew that is a rare treat. It is a rich stew. This recipe serves 4.

● A quahog or quahaug, if you prefer that spelling, is a hard-shelled round clam. Large quahogs are known as "Chowders," medium-sized quahogs are called "Cherry-stones" and small quahogs are "Littlenecks." It is cherrystones and littlnecks that taste so good "on the halfshell." They're just the right size for eating raw.

Quahog Stew

½ cup butter
1 pint shucked quahogs with liquor
1 quart milk or 3 cups milk and 1 cup light cream
¼ teaspoon black pepper
½ teaspoon salt

Scald the milk. While it is heating, melt the butter in a saucepan. Add the raw quahogs, which have been chopped fine, and the liquor to the melted butter. Cut up the quahogs by placing them on a small wooden board and with a paring knife cut each one into several small pieces. Simmer the butter, chopped raw quahogs and liquor together about 3 minutes. Add to heated milk. Add salt and pepper. Taste, to be sure of seasoning. Serve at once with crackers. Serves 4.

Quahog stew can be made in exactly the same way if you use steamed quahogs. In other words, if you have steamed the quahogs to open them, then remove the cooked quahogs from the shells and chop the quahogs into small pieces. Use about ½ cup of the broth with the chopped quahogs in the melted butter and simmer this all together for 3 minutes, before adding it to the heated milk.

Quahogs are excellent used in a chowder, and it is made exactly as you would make clam chowder; just be sure you chop the quahogs before adding them to the chowder.

● You will find parsnips in our markets almost year round. I like them best when a neighbor or friend lets them stay in his garden all winter, then digs them to share as a very special part of springtime in Maine. They're almost as good as dandelion or fiddlehead greens. Keep in mind that parsnips have a sweet flavor.

Parsnip Stew

2 slices salt pork(or use 2 tablespoons margarine)
1 small onion, diced
2 cups diced potatoes
2 cups water
Salt and pepper to taste
3 cups parsnips, cut in cubes
1 quart milk
4 tablespoons margarine

We say, "try out" salt pork. It means to cook slowly, using a low heat. Remove pieces of pork, add onion and cook gently. You may favor using margarine; in that case cook onion in it. Add diced potatoes, water, salt and pepper; cover kettle, bring to steaming point. Cook potatoes 10 minutes, then add cubed parsnips which do not take as long to cook. Return cover and cook for 10 minutes, after steaming point is again reached. Test for doneness and add milk. Season to taste. Add margarine or butter, if it has not been used in place of salt pork. Some cooks like to add ½ cup rolled out cracker crumbs for thickening. Serve bowls of Parsnip Stew topped with minced parsley. This recipe serves 6.

Oyster Stew

1 pint oysters
1½ pints to 1 quart milk
6 tablespoons butter
1 tablespoon Worcestershire sauce
½ teaspoon celery salt
Salt to season, after stew is made
½ to 1 teaspoon paprika

Put raw oysters in saucepan. Add butter and seasonings. Stir and bring quickly to a boil, lower heat, continue stirring and cooking not longer than 2 minutes, allowing edges of oysters to curl. Add milk, bring again to just below boiling point, but do not allow to boil (or it could curdle). Dip into bowls, add another piece of butter to each bowl if you wish, sprinkle with paprika. Serve with oyster crackers. This serves 2 amply. If you use a quart of milk it will serve 4 skimpily.

Biscuits & Muffins

Perfect Blueberry Muffins

2 cups flour
½ teaspoon salt
3 teaspoons baking powder
1 cup milk
2 teaspoons lemon juice
1 well beaten egg
¼ cup salad oil
⅓ cup sugar
¾ cup blueberries

Sift flour, salt, baking powder and sugar together. Beat egg well, add milk. Stir in oil and lemon juice. Add liquid to dry ingredients. Stir about 20 seconds. Flour should be all dampened, but mixture should still be lumpy. When just a few patches of flour are left, fold in blueberries, gently. Fill greased muffin tins two-thirds full. Bake at 425 degrees for about 25 minutes.

● Chances are this is the recipe for graham gems your grandmother used, too. Of course, she baked them in her heavy black iron gem pan.

Graham Gems

1½ cups graham flour
3 tablespoons sugar
1 teaspoon salt
1 teaspoon soda
3 tablespoons molasses
1 cup sour milk or buttermilk

Mix in order given. The graham flour is not sifted. Measure by spoonfuls into cup. Turn into mixing bowl. Add sugar, salt and soda. Mix well, then add molasses and buttermilk or sour milk.

There are no eggs in this recipe. Turn into gem pans or muffin tins. Bake at 400 degrees for about 25 minutes.

Squash Muffins

1 egg
¼ cup sugar
½ cup milk
½ cup cooked mashed squash
1¾ cups flour
2 teaspoons cream of tartar
1 teaspoon soda
½ teaspoon salt
4 tablespoons melted shortening or oil

Beat egg and sugar, add milk and squash. Sift flour, measure and sift with dry ingredients. Combine with beaten egg mixture. Do this lightly. Add shortening. Turn into greased muffin tins.

Bake at 375 degrees for about 20 minutes. Makes 12 muffins.

Buttermilk Biscuits

2 cups flour
1 teaspoon salt
4 teaspoons baking powder
½ teaspoon soda
5 tablespoons shortening
¾ cup buttermilk
approximately

Sift flour and measure. Sift with salt, baking powder and soda.

Cut in shortening, using pastry blender or 2 knives. Add buttermilk to make a soft dough, stirring quickly.

Turn onto floured board, knead this dough for one minute. Roll ½ inch thick. Cut, using floured biscuit cutter.

Place on ungreased baking sheet. Let pan of biscuits stand 30 minutes at room temperature. Bake at 450 degrees for about 15 minutes.

This particular recipe for biscuits may be mixed in the morning, placed on the baking sheet, covered and placed in the refrigerator to be baked at night. Let come to room temperature before baking.

Twin Mountain Muffins

2 cups sifted flour
3 teaspoons baking powder
½ teaspoon salt
2 tablespoons sugar
1 cup milk
2 tablespoons melted butter or vegetable oil
1 egg, well beaten

Sift flour, measure and sift together with baking powder, salt and sugar. Combine egg, milk and melted butter or oil. Turn into dry ingredients, mixing only enough to dampen flour. Spoon into greased muffin pans. Makes 12 muffins. Bake at 400 degrees for 25 minutes.

Actually these are plain muffins, and if you want to make true Twin Mountain Muffins, you double the amount of sugar and butter or oil.

These muffins will provide a built-in breakfast and will be popular in your family.

Maple Muffins

2 cups flour, sifted
4 teaspoons baking powder
½ teaspoon salt
1 egg
½ cup milk
½ cup maple syrup
¼ cup vegetable oil

Sift dry ingredients together into a bowl. Combine egg, slightly beaten with milk, maple syrup and oil. Add liquid to dry ingredients. Mix gently. Spoon into greased muffins tins. Makes 12 muffins. Bake at 400 degrees for 18 to 20 minutes.

● Cheese and bacon muffins disappear "like mist before the sun" when they appear in the Coffee Shop at the Augusta General Hospital on Wednesday mornings. It is a privilege to have this recipe to share with you from the Coffee Shop volunteer who originated this recipe. It would not be unusual, for she is that kind of a cook.

Cheese and Bacon Muffins

**Fry ¼ to ⅓ pound bacon, depending
upon its leanness
Reserve ⅓ cup of the drippings
1 egg
1 cup milk
1 cup sharp cheese, shredded
2 cups flour, sifted
1 teaspoon salt
¼ cup sugar
3 teaspons baking powder**

Beat egg slightly, stir in milk, the ⅓ cup bacon fat and 1 cup shredded cheese. Set aside. Sift together the flour, salt, sugar and baking powder. Stir into the egg mixture. Crumble the fried bacon and add to mixture. Spoon into greased muffin tins. Bake at 400 degrees for 18 to 20 minutes. Makes 12 muffins.

● It is not hard to recall the very first time I ever ate these biscuits — it was a hot summer's night and they were served with a salad. It has been many years since this family lived in Augusta but I like to think of the fine gift our hostess left us by sharing her unusual biscuit recipe. I say this because it has three leavening agents — soda, cream of tartar and baking powder. I make these biscuits when I have buttermilk on hand.

This reminds me. If you have an old-fashioned recipe calling for sour milk, you realize, of course, that you may substitute an equal amount of buttermilk. If you are without either, then add 1 tablespoon of vinegar or lemon juice to 1 cup of sweet milk.

Buttermilk Biscuits

2 cups sifted flour
¼ teaspoon salt
1 teaspoon soda
2 teaspoons cream of tartar
1½ teaspoons baking powder
2 rounded tablespoons shortening
1 cup buttermilk

Sift flour, measure and sift together with salt, soda, cream of tartar and baking powder.

Cut in the shortening, using a pastry blender or 2 knives. Add the buttermilk quickly, using a fork for stirring into dry ingredients. Knead lightly on a floured board.

Cut in size biscuits desired, place on a greased pan and bake at 475 degrees for 10 to 12 minutes.

● This recipe is made with yeast as well as buttermilk, so you have a great flavor combined with lightness and a simple procedure for making this hot bread, for there is no rising of the dough. Best of all, it makes 3 dozen.

Angel Biscuits

1 yeast cake or 1 envelope dry yeast
2 tablespoons lukewarm water
5 cups flour, unsifted
¼ cup sugar
2 teaspoons baking powder
1 teaspoon soda
1 teaspoon salt
1 cup shortening
2 cups buttermilk

Dissolve yeast in lukewarm water and let stand 5 minutes.

Measure flour into cup by spoonfuls. Sift flour, sugar, baking powder, soda and salt. Using pastry blender or 2 knives, cut shortening into sifted dry ingredients. Add buttermilk and dissolved yeast and mix well. Turn onto floured board, knead 2 or 3 times, roll to desired thickness. Cut into biscuits, dip into melted margarine. Fold over like Parker House rolls or place flat biscuits in greased pan.

Bake at 450 degrees for 12 minutes. This recipe makes 3 dozen regular size biscuits. If you do not want to bake all at once, place in 2 pans, one for baking now. Slide the other unbaked into a plastic bag, seal, place in freezer for baking at a later time. When you do this, bring to room temperature, which will allow the biscuits to thaw, then bake as in directions.

● A muffin recipe that has swept the state, so to speak, is a delicious muffin. But best of all, the large amount of batter is mixed then stored in the refrigerator, tightly covered, for up to six weeks time. An Augusta friend brought the recipe to me a few years ago when she returned from Florida.

Best-Of-Mine Muffins

2 cups All-Bran
2 cups boiling water
1 cup, plus 3 tablespoons vegetable shortening
2½ cups sugar
4 eggs
1 quart buttermilk
4 cups Bran-Buds
6 cups flour, sifted
5 teaspoons soda
2 teaspoons salt

Pour boiling water over All-Bran and allow to set while mixing ingredients. Cream shortening and sugar. Add eggs one at a time, beating well after each addition. Blend in the quart of buttermilk. Add All-Bran and water mixture. Add the 4 cups of Bran-Buds.

Sift flour together with soda and salt. Add to mixture. Turn into large container and cover tightly. Keep refrigerated for up to 6 weeks. Do not stir. Merely spoon into muffin tins as you get ready to bake muffins. Bake at 400 degrees for 16 to 20 minutes or until top is firm.

My Mother's Cream of Tartar Biscuits

2 cups sifted flour
5 teaspoons cream of tartar
2 teaspoons soda
½ teaspoon salt
Piece of vegetable shortening, size of an egg
Milk — to make a stiff batter

Sift flour, soda, cream of tartar and salt into a bowl. Cut in shortening, using a pastry blender or two knives for this. Add milk, using a fork to mix until just the last of the flour disappears and the dough seems just right for rolling and cutting into biscuits.

Turn dough onto lightly floured surface, handle very little, only enough to mold into shape and flatten by patting with your fingers or rolling to about 1-inch thickness.

Dip a biscuit cutter into flour and cut biscuits, placing on greased baking sheet, a dot of butter or margarine on each biscuit helps before putting in oven at 450 degrees for about 10 to 12 minutes.

Cranberry Muffins

1 cup chopped raw cranberries
½ cup sugar
2 cups sifted flour
¼ teaspoon salt
¾ teaspoon soda
¼ cup sugar
1 egg, slightly beaten
¾ cup sour milk or buttermilk
4 tablespoons melted shortening

Using a chopping bowl and chopping knife, chop the raw cranberries. Measure 1 cup, combine with the ½ cup sugar, set aside.

Measure sifted flour and sift together with salt, soda and the ¼ cup sugar. Sift into mixing bowl. Beat 1 egg slightly, combine with sour milk or buttermilk and melted shortening. Add to dry ingredients, mix lightly until flour disappears. Gently fold in the chopped cranberry mixture. Fill greased muffin tins two-thirds full. Makes 12 muffins. Bake at 400 degrees for 20 minutes.

Doughnut Muffins

1 egg
1/3 cup cooking oil
1/2 cup milk
1 1/2 cups flour
2 teaspoons baking powder
1/2 teaspoon salt
1/2 teaspoon nutmeg
1/2 cup sugar

Using a fork, beat egg in mixing bowl. Add oil and milk. Continue beating with fork. Sift flour, measure and sift with sugar, baking powder, salt and nutmeg. Add to mixture and stir with fork, very lightly. Turn into 12 greased muffin tins. This will make 12 medium-sized muffins. Sprinkle each muffin with a mixture of sugar and cinnamon and put a dot of butter or margarine on top of each. Bake at 400 degrees about 20 minutes.

Bran Muffins

1 cup whole bran cereal
1 cup sifted flour
1/4 cup sugar
3 teaspoons baking powder
1/2 teaspoon salt
1 egg
1 cup milk
1/4 cup vegetable oil

Sift flour, sugar, baking powder and salt into a bowl. Stir in the bran cereal. In a medium bowl and using a fork, beat the egg slightly, add milk and oil. Add egg mixture all at once to flour mixture. Using a spoon, stir until flour is moistened. The batter will be lumpy. Spoon into greased muffin tins. Makes 12 muffins. Bake at 400 degrees for 25 minutes until golden brown.

Oatmeal Muffins

Soak 2 cups oatmeal or rolled oats in
1⅔ cups milk for 2 hours
Add:
1 tablespoon melted shortening or oil
1 beaten egg
Add sifted dry ingredients:
1 cup flour
½ cup sugar
½ teaspoon salt
2 level teaspoons cream of tartar
1 heaping teaspoon soda

Makes about 18 muffins. Bake at 400 degrees for 20 minutes.

Good Gravy

A break in this cookbook between Chowders Soups and Stews and the second section called "Good Gravy" is a column I wrote years ago. It is a nostalgic column. During the 25 years I wrote Cooking Down East, a weekly column in the Maine Sunday Telegram, I had many favorites. This is one of them. It had to be for it was written about my family. It is lovingly printed just as I wrote it, recipes and all. These are excellent recipes. I did not update them.

As you drive over the bridge at Bath, do you ever think of the days when the only way of crossing the Kennebec River at that point was by ferry? The time I remember best about taking the ferry was after Dad had bought our first car. It was a Model-T. That was exciting in itself, but when he told us we were going to take a Sunday trip, Doris and I could hardly wait for the day to arrive.

We lived at New Meadows.

This was no ordinary excursion for the Holbrooks, as we learned we were going to Bath, and we'd take the early morning ferry. Best of all, once on the Woolwich side of the Kennebec, we were going to cook breakfast by the roadside.

Last summer when I was talking with my mother about that day long ago, she remembered that I whistled all day long, which must have been aggravating.

The area was not built-up along the highway as it is now in Woolwich. It was at this time of the year: haying was done and the fields at the side of the road were just the spot for cooking breakfast.

After leaving the ferry we soon found a good place.

The Sterno stove was lighted and bacon and eggs were fried. Coffee for Mother and Dad was no problem for it had been made at the farm at New Meadows and was in a thermos bottle. None of us ever forgot how good breakfast tasted in the clear, cool air of an early Maine morning, so long ago.

That was only part of the trip, for we went into Wiscasset, on to Randolph, over the bridge, and home through Bowdoinham along the River Road. It was a family joke that if Dad took us on a ride it was sure to include a view of Merrymeeting Bay. He was apt to say, "Let's ride up to the Bay." We never questioned which bay he meant.

Chances are, we did not take this trip until the "garden stuff" was taken care of. Like all mothers of that era, mine put up endless jars of string beans, shell beans, tomatoes, and there were sure to be pickles in the making. You just didn't go on picnics until this was all done.

With this in mind, how is your own "garden stuff" coming along? Last summer, Mrs. Frank W. Haines of Augusta gave me her method for making tomato juice cocktail which you are sure to like.

Mrs. Frank W. Haines' Tomato Cocktail

3 quarts tomatoes, measured after cutting up
2 quarts water
½ cup sugar
6 tablespoons chopped onions
3 tablespoons salt
½ teaspoon pepper
12 whole cloves

Mix all together and boil gently for 45 minutes. Put through strainer or food mill. Simmer 10 minutes. Seal. Makes 2 quarts and 1 pint.

The two recipes below, used many years by Mrs. Joseph Baumann of Lisbon Falls, are now used by her daughters and all their friends.

Mrs. Baumann's Dill Pickles

3 quarts water
1 quart vinegar
1 cup salt (heaped a little)

Try to get salt without cornstarch added. We used to call it "bag salt."
Bring to boil, pour over washed and dried cucumbers packed in quart jar. (Place one stalk dill in bottom of jar, one on top.) Seal.

Dilled String Beans

Use a pint jar, 1 stalk dill in bottom. Cook string beans with only ends snapped off, in salted water for 15 minutes or until tender. Drain. Fill jar. Pour hot liquid over. Seal.

Good Gravy

Several years ago a young woman in Augusta called often with questions about cooking. I never met her, nor can I remember her name, but once she said, "Marjorie, if you ever write another cookbook, you should call it "Good Gravy."

I asked why and found if I was puzzled about a cooking question, I would say "Good Gravy," so here it is.

This will be a collection that I have not used before. What comes first? My favorite recipe, Baked Chicken Sandwiches.

This recipe makes 10 sandwiches which are prepared and wrapped in foil, placed in the freezer for later use.

They are prepared in the following manner.

Baked Chicken Sandwiches
(Serves 10)

Use a loaf of sandwich bread. The filling is prepared as follows:

2 cups chicken breasts, diced
1 can cream of mushroom soup
1 can Franco-American chicken gravy
2 tablespoons diced pimiento
2 tablespoons minced onion
1 can sliced water chestnuts, drained
green pepper, diced small, if desired

Mix together. Place in refrigerator for an hour, to blend flavors. This will be soupy, but when ready to make sandwiches, ignore this.

Make 10 sandwiches. I prefer Pepperidge Farm sandwich bread.

Use all of filling, spreading evenly on each of the 10 sandwiches. Place on cookie sheet in freezer, when frozen, wrap each sandwich in foil and place in freezer. These will keep for several weeks.

To prepare for baking and serving, for 10 sandwiches use 4 eggs, beaten slightly with 2 to 4 tablespoons milk.

Unwrap sandwiches and drop each frozen sandwich or number you intend using in egg and milk.

Use rolled out cereal for crumbs. Place on cookie

sheet for baking. Bake one hour at 300. Serve with the following sauce:

1 8 oz. package cream cheese
1 stick margarine.

Heated in top of double boiler. Cut down on amount if fewer sandwiches are being cooked. Beat together to make smooth, add small amount cold milk, if needed.

Place sandwich on plate, spoon small amount of sauce on each sandwich. Decorate with sprig of parsley.

● This recipe for Mock Lobster Salad given to me by Josephine Trafton who cooked for the Lions Club in Gardiner, Maine, has met with great approval.

Mock Lobster Salad

2 pounds haddock
1 medium onion, sliced
¾ cup commercial sour cream
½ cup chili sauce
2 to 3 tablespoons horseradish
1 to 2 tablespoons mayonnaise
salt to taste
1 tablespoon fresh lemon juice
2 cups diced celery

Simmer fish in two cups salted water with sliced onion until fish is white, about 5 minutes. Drain and cool. Flake fish in large pieces. Add celery, diced small.

Combine commercial sour cream, chili sauce, horseradish, mayonnaise and lemon juice. Blend well with fish. Refrigerate. Stir well before serving, blending lightly. Serve on lettuce with a light dusting of paprika. Serves 8.

● If you have not made Garden Pea Casserole, then this has to be the time to make this delicious casserole to serve with any chicken recipe.

Garden Pea Casserole

2 1-pound pkgs. frozen peas
1 stick margarine
4 slices onion, minced
¼ cup slivered almonds, chopped
1 can cream of mushroom soup
About ½ cup buttered crumbs

Cook peas, drain. Melt margarine. Add minced onion, cook over low heat. Add nuts. Cook slowly. Add soup. Mix with cooked drained peas. Turn into buttered casserole. Top with buttered crumbs. Bake at 350 degrees for 20 minutes. Do not overcook. Serves 8. This may be prepared the day before serving. Bring to room temperature. Then cook for 20 minutes.

● The following cranberry salad will add tartness to this luncheon.

Easy Cranberry Salad

1 3-oz. pkg. raspberry gelatin
1 cup boiling water
¾ cup cold water

Mix raspberry gelatin with boiling water, stirring until dissolved. Add cold water, mixing well. Place in refrigerator until this starts to jell.

Add one 14-oz. jar cranberry orange relish and ½ cup chopped walnuts. Spoon into custard cups or use one large salad mold.

Serve with lettuce and top with mayonnaise.

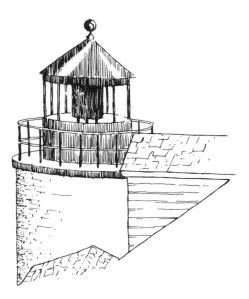

● Cracker Snackers, to serve at parties, is a popular, easily prepared recipe. Stored in a tightly covered tin, these crackers will keep for weeks.

Cracker Snackers

1 11-oz. envelope Ranch-style salad dressing mix (use dry)
¼ teaspoon whole dill weed
¼ teaspoon lemon pepper
⅛ teaspoon garlic powder
2 11-oz. pkg. oyster crackers
½ cup vegetable oil

Combine first four ingredients in a bowl. Add crackers. Toss well to distribute seasonings over all. Drizzle oil over crackers, mixing well. Turn mixture into a large paper bag. Fold top to close bag securely. Let stand 2 hours shaking bag occasionally. When time is up, turn into tightly covered container.
  Yields 11½ cups.

If you have not made white chocolate candy, then you are in for a treat.

White Chocolate Candy

1 pound white chocolate
1 cup cocktail peanuts or walnuts
2 cups thin pretzels, broken in half once

Melt chocolate in top of double boiler. Stir into bowl of peanuts and pretzels. Spread on wax paper on counter. When cool, break into pieces.
Makes 4 half-pound boxes.

Heath Chips — also a candy — is a favorite with many. It's another easy-to-make recipe.

Heath Chips — A Candy

Use a large jelly roll pan. Line it with foil. "Butter" the foil. Lay 40 saltines in rows on the foil. In a saucepan melt:
2 sticks margarine
Add 1 cup firmly-packed light brown sugar

Bring to a boil. Boil just 3 minutes. Pour this syrup all over the saltines. Place pan in a 400-degree oven. Bake exactly 5 minutes.
Place pan on rack to cool. Sprinkle one 12-oz. pkg. chocolate bits all over the syrup. Spread evenly all over saltines. Sprinkle chopped nuts over top. When cool, place in refrigerator. When these are hard, break up. Store in freezer or refrigerator.

Notes ~

Notes ~